DOCTORS

Written By:
Herbert I. Kavet

Illustrated By:
Martin Riskin

© 1993
by **Ivory Tower Publishing Company, Inc.**
All Rights Reserved

No portion of this book may be reproduced - mechanically, electronically, or by any other means including photocopying - without the permission of the publisher.

Manufactured in the United States of America

30 29 28 27 26 25 24 23 22 21 20 19 18 17 16 15 14 13 12 11 10 9 8 7 6 5 4 3 2 1

Ivory Tower Publishing Co., Inc.
125 Walnut Street
P.O. Box 9132
Watertown, MA 02272-9132
Telephone #: (617) 923-1111   Fax #: (617) 923-8839

Offshore Medical School

The image of offshore medical schools as havens for students unable to get into real medical schools is, of course, ridiculous. Many of the students choosing schools in Grenada and Mexico have attended fully accredited high schools, and many even graduated from college. These doctors just recognize the importance of sun tans and surfing as part of the human body's overall well-being and image of a successful physician.

Some of the imaginative procedures from these schools have even found their way into mainstream medical practice.

Everyone Wants To Play Doctor

Every physical therapist, chiropractor, psychologist, masseur and dietician thinks they can practice medicine, and are all horning in on the profession. It's no wonder malpractice insurance has gotten so expensive with all these imposters trying to cure people. Give them a sharp knife and a good painkiller and they'd be performing brain surgery.

Chiropractors

No matter what the ailment, the chiropractor always says the same thing to their patients. "There's an alignment problem in your back. Now this has been going on for a long time, but I can correct it. It's going to take some time, of course, to do the adjustments so you've got to commit to a program of visits." Then he tells you–in a conspiratorial tone–that one leg is 3/8" longer than the other. It's best to pick a chiropractor whose office is close by and with easy parking, because these visits go on for the rest of your life.

Saturday Morning At The Emergency Room

They call them handymen because they lose their hands so often. Mostly fingers, actually, and horrible lacerations. The emergency rooms are full of them every Saturday morning, as the unskilled masses of paper pushers play carpenter and gardener for the weekend. If they would broadcast football games during this time slot, 40% of the hospitals in the country would be forced to close.

"HOW LONG WILL IT BE BEFORE HE CAN FINISH THE GUTTERS?"

Second Opinions

All these magazine articles tell patients to seek second opinions. No one does unless they don't like the first opinion, after which the patient seeks third and fourth opinions until he or she finds one more to their liking. The reason it's so hard to get an appointment with a specialist is that each one diagnoses the same disease an average of 2.6 times.

Psychiatrists

All the weirdos and sickest students from college seem to gravitate to the study of psychiatry. This is just as well, since you'd rather not have these people messing with bodies and cutting or prescribing. Every doctor remembers the psychiatry students from their med-school days and thanks God that they have chosen a specialty where they can't do too much damage.

Psychiatry & Psychology

The only people crazier than psychiatrists are psychologists. Psychologists haven't even really gotten an education. They slip through some Junior College, perhaps manage a mail-order doctorate, hang out a shingle, and pretend to be a physician for the rest of their life. A dangerous group, indeed, who will assiduously avoid you at parties.

Psychiatrists and Wealth

$100 an hour for a fifty minute session is a tough way to build a fortune. Incidentally, the extra ten minutes are used by psychiatrists to go into the bathroom and practice looking sage in front of the mirror. To build a real fortune as a psychiatrist, you have to write a best-selling book, which most of them do, except those that can't spell. Hearing those great stories all day and just sitting there with a pad and pencil makes this easy.

Pagers

Pagers used to be fun and a useful, prestigious calling device, but that was before every tradesman and teenager carried them. A beeper going off in a crowd now-a-days draws sneers and accusations of being a drug dealer, which may not be far off the mark. The kind that vibrates rather than makes a noise will cause you the least embarrassment.

"EXCUSE ME, THIS MUST BE MY PAROLE OFFICER."

Pagers And Sex

1. Pagers are responsible for the majority of divorces amongst doctors.
2. Pagers are a cause of frigidity in 62% of all doctors' wives.
3. Pagers are an excuse for premature ejaculation in 47% of all doctors' husbands.

Interns And Residents

No one knows why interns and residents are paid so little and work so hard. This final initiation into the world of practicing medicine is potentially the most dangerous to patients. The fact is, few patients are seriously misdiagnosed or injured by sleepy interns and residents, which is either a tribute to the stamina of youth or a testimonial to the recuperative powers of the human body.

Surgeons, Internists and Pathologists

1. The Internist knows everything, but does nothing.
2. The Surgeon knows nothing, but does everything.
3. The Pathologist knows everything and does everything, but it's too late.

Drug Samples

The federal government and national consumer groups deplore rising drug prices, and every doctor knows the real reason behind these escalating costs. Drug samples. Open any drawer in any doctor's office and it's crammed full of samples. After fiddling with insurance and medicare forms, sorting, storing and keeping track of expiration dates on samples is the single most pressing problem in medicine today.

Drug Abuses

There are all these drugs and other controlled substances out in the wonderful world that make people feel real good. Perhaps too good, because if somebody didn't control these overly happy people, they probably wouldn't bother going to work and would forget to pay taxes, and their Visa bills, not to mention medical insurance. So the government (Republicans more than Democrats), which is very concerned about these things, decided to put doctors in charge of distributing these drugs. It probably has something to do with doctors being the only segment of the population smart enough to spell all those long drug names.

"TELL ME AGAIN, WHY YOU NEED A PRESCRIPTION FOR DEMEROL."

Ear, Nose and Throat Specialists

Many think these doctors are drawn from groups of people who couldn't get into dental schools. Some others think these specialists just prefer a branch of medicine that doesn't involve too much bending over. There is no question about the dedication of Ear, Nose and Throat physicians when you think of all the things you can pick up poking about in people's mouths and ear wax. Most flu epidemics, it's a fact, start amongst these doctors when they forget to wash their hands. When one of these physicians figures out a way to control the growth of hair in ears and nostrils, he or she is going to make a fortune.

Proctologists

I'm not going to succumb to the usual temptation to poke fun at this end of the medical profession. These physicians, after all, are just as dedicated as, say, dermatologists, and study long and hard to maintain the health and well-being of the posteriors of our nation. There is absolutely nothing abnormal about Proctologists, and the fact that these groups account for over 70% of the sales of our FART books, is probably just a coincidence.

Psychiatrists

"Real doctors" may look down their noses at these purveyors of mental aid but, in truth, they have chosen one of the more difficult specialities. No other branch of medicine is so besieged by amateurs who have taken a sophomore course in psychology, and are ready to practice on their friends and family. And no other branch of medicine has to deal with certifiable crazies all day. Regular doctors get their share of nuts, but at least they are interspersed with some normal people. Moreover, it's hard to determine results with psychiatry. You can pretty much tell when a heart, liver, or limb is healed, but heads are harder to see into, and the weirdos who visit psychiatrists are used to lying all the time.

3 years of psychiatric visits finally taught Phyllis to feel comfortable when introducing friends to her family.

Psychiatrists and Sexual Harassment

Why are psychiatrists always involved with sexual harassment problems?

1. There's a couch in their office.
2. They encourage patients to talk about their most intimate behavior.
3. Psychiatrists, on the whole, are one of the horniest groups of people in the world due to #2.

Doctors at Parties

Clever physicians pretend to sell insurance or securities, or do something vague in research when at a social gathering. If that doesn't work, the doctor must pretty much resign her- or himself to hearing descriptions of operations and prescribing remedies for back ailments all evening.

"IF THAT DOESN'T WORK, HERE'S THE NAME OF A SPECIALIST WHO'LL BE AT THE FINSTERBERG PARTY FRIDAY NIGHT."

Doctors at Parties

The best way to avoid practicing medicine all evening is to attend parties where most of the other guests are also doctors. Then, however, you will have to put up with the shop talk from all the other doctors and the endless bitching about the latest government interference in medicine.

Lawyers and Doctors

Lawyers used to be perceived by physicians as allied, highly intelligent and well-educated professionals who just couldn't stand the sight of blood. But the explosion of malpractice suits has forever ended this relationship. Doctors, like much of the rest of the population, regard lawyers as money-grubbing jackals, bent on destroying western civilization as we know it. It's hard to find anyone these days to argue with this.

Lawyers and Doctors

Lawyers often try to improve their terrible relationship with doctors by offering them lucrative deals to sit around in courtrooms all day waiting to give expert testimony. While this can be amusing the first few times, doctors are not used to having their opinions challenged, and this is just what the opposing lawyer is paid to do. Worse, this lawyer will call in more medical experts and one may be your old professor.

"ATTORNEY FLENIBECK WOULD LIKE ONE MORE ASSURANCE THAT YOU WON'T USE THE RUSTY SCALPEL YOU THREATENED HIM WITH IN COURT LAST WEEK."

Keeping Up-To-Date

Medical conferences are one of the best ways to keep up-to-date, and there is no reason why you can't learn on a sunny beach, or ski slope, as well as in Hoboken, New Jersey. The I.R.S. understands this and encourages medical conferences by making them fully tax deductible. Besides, a tan doctor is a healthy, confidence-inspiring doctor.

Dr. Flengle recognized the importance of keeping informed on all the latest developments in his field and promised himself he'd read the journals he'd been saving the first rainy weekend.

Disgusting Procedures

Every now and then a doctor is obligated to perform a really terrible procedure. I'm not going to write descriptions here, but to make sure your partners and family know what you go through for them, you owe it to yourself to describe and discuss these procedures in all their gruesome details. Meal times are always a good occasion for this.

"TAKE A MEMO, MS FORESNIP, I WANT TO SEE THOSE MED STUDENTS FIRST THING TOMORROW MORNING."

Nobody Wants To Grow Old

Years ago, as people aged, they would slow down. They would grow stout and sit in chairs and relive the exploits of their youth. The fitness craze has changed all that and stressed orthopedic doctors all out of proportion to the rest of the medical profession. These 40-year-old athletes don't just want the injured bone set, they want to go back into the rugby game that afternoon. The 50-year-old woman who has her knee blown out on a ski slope expects to be doing Nastar races by the end of the season. Rest and taking it easy used to be the treatment of choice by 75% of all orthopedic doctors, but now they have to work for their fees.

Surgeons and Carving

Surgeons are always asked to carve the turkey when they are at other people's homes for Thanksgiving and other holidays. If they don't actually get the job, whoever does carve will usually kid the surgeon with comments like, "How am I doing, Doc?" or "Do you really get $20,000 for this kind of work?" You can shut them up by saying, "Taking them apart is easy. It's the putting them back together that's the hard part."

When Surgeons Need Surgery

This is the acid test of medicine, and all doctors know how badly it fails. When you see the terror on the face of a surgeon who needs a little surgery, you wonder what these guys know that the rest of us don't. You've all heard them saying, "Well, if I ever need surgery no one will touch me but Williams." What about the other 23 surgeons in the hospital? Can they all have shaky hands and short attention spans?

"...I'll get to your artery as soon as I finish shaving Alf."

The Examining Room Fart

Why is it, so often when you go into the examining room, the patient has just farted and is self-consciously wafting the air around trying to dissipate the odor? Is it the gown with the opening in the back that encourages this behavior? Perhaps they are nervous or we keep them waiting too long and this is their revenge. Regardless, it gets the examination off to a tense start and in extreme cases, causes your eyes to water so much that you can hardly read their blood pressure.

Doctor Farts

People think, for some reason, that doctors don't fart. This makes it incredibly easy, when you blast a big one, to pass the blame to some bystanders or even to the totally innocent and bewildered patient. "Well, Mrs. Feldstein, have you been having some gastric distress?" "No, no," she'll say, but not with the total conviction that she didn't give birth to that major stinker after all. Women doctors, of course, never fart.

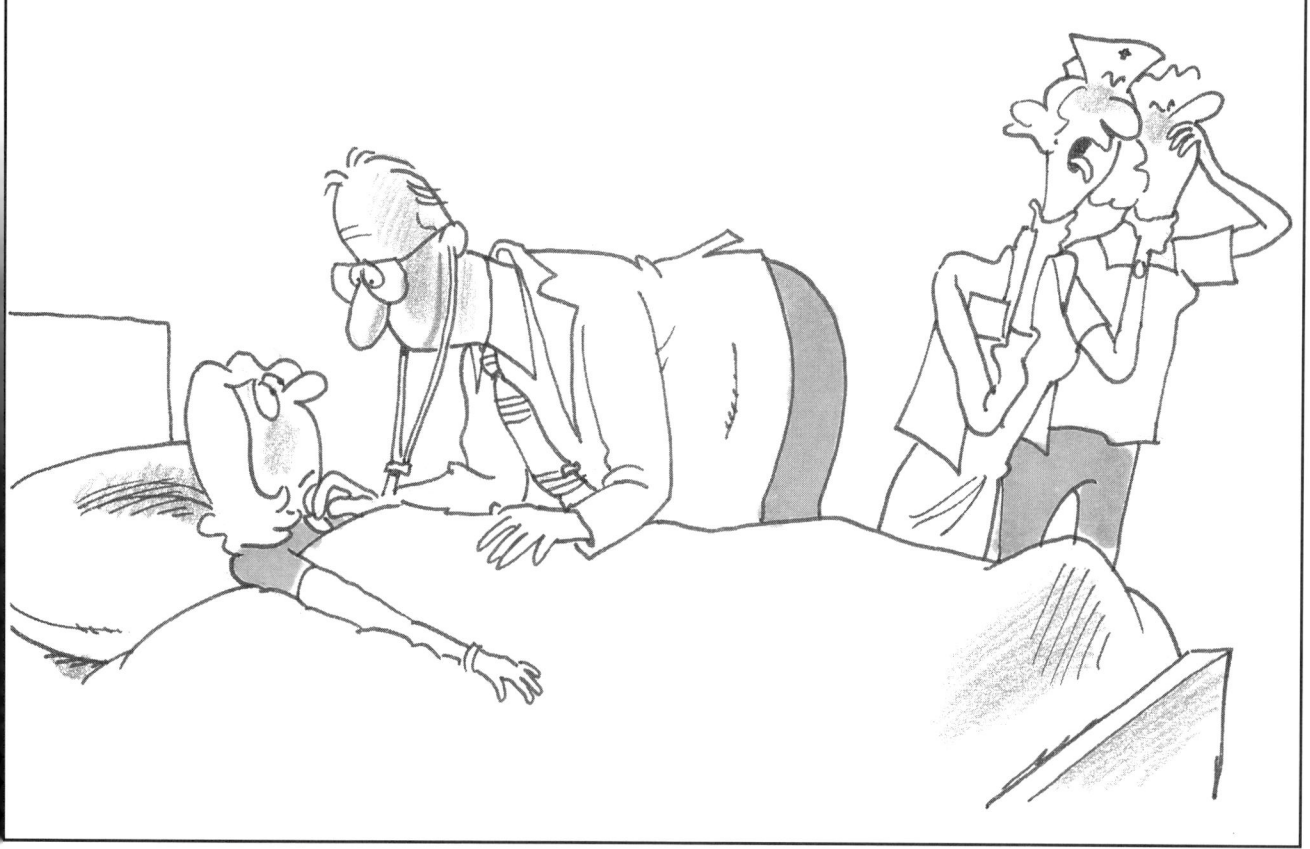

Unnecessary Procedures

Patients pretty much get better no matter what you do, but doing nothing leaves them terribly unsatisfied. Here they've taken off time from work to see you and paid the $2 for the HMO and, by God, they want some treatment. The real skill in medicine comes from knowing what to do or prescribe that will satisfy your patient's wants without interfering too much with the natural healing process.

Bathroom Surgery

It's bad enough competing will all the pseudo-doctors practicing under names like Podiatrist, Chiropractor and physical therapist, but the pure gall of having to compete with their own patients drives many doctors to despair. After health insurance, bathroom surgery is the biggest problem in medicine today. You have all these potential patients treating themselves with tweezers, needles and other assorted instruments, poking about splinters, squeezing pimples, fiddling with ingrown toenails and God knows what else. Worse, they do it in front of a mirror where everything is backwards.

Bathroom Surgery

These bathroom activities can cause endless infections and permanent disfigurement. Do the insurance companies try to control this mockery of medicine? No, because they don't get any paperwork on it. They wait until you correct the problem in a proper antiseptic method, and then they yell at you about the cost.

Mom as Doctor

This unlicensed practitioner of medicine really bears watching. Some of the embarrassing manifestations of Moms practicing medicine are:

1. Prescribes old folk remedies (like chicken soup) which usually work.
2. Makes house calls.
3. Can be reached at any hour and doesn't use a beeper.
4. Continues to advise you and her other patients (no matter how prominent you've become) and constantly follows up.
5. Sends her sick friends to you, but doesn't expect you to charge them.

Mom as Doctor

These mothers, of course, do have a few weaknesses that show their lack of formal training.

1. She specializes in where the patient caught the cold rather than how to cure it.
2. She spends an inordinate amount of time with questions about nutrition and warm clothes.
3. Often cuts off discussion with "I told you so."
4. She thinks she knows everything but never does tests.
5. She keeps current by reading women's magazines and watching "20/20."

Giving Patients Bad News

No joking here, this is one of the toughest parts about being a doctor. The patient may have been smoking three packs a day, living on M&M's and bacon, and risen from his TV chair only to open a beer, but it's still hard to tell them bad news. Here is where second opinions and psychological counsellors come to your aid.

How to Act Like a Country Doctor

In the era of more and more specialization, a small movement has started to glorify the old-fashioned country family doctor. Here's how to be a hit with the granola crowd by pretending to be one!

1. Keep lots of lollipops for the kids and suck one yourself on occasion. <u>Little House on the Prairie</u> books are good, too.
2. Drive an old car, preferably a Ford.
3. If you have a receptionist or nurse, make sure her name is Agnes or Fanny.
4. Eschew wearing ties and jackets.
5. Instead of writing prescriptions, give the patient a jar of something you "whipped up."

Sex Problems

All sex problems that patients come to you with can be divided into two categories:

1. Those they are too embarrassed to talk about.
2. Those, once they get started, they won't shut up about.

It's amazing how quickly they switch from embarrassment to loquaciousness with such little encouragement—now you know where psychiatrists get all their great stories for parties.

Sex Problems

Once they start talking about sex, it's often hard to get them to shut up. Everyone loves talking about sex, especially to a supposed expert who is sworn to confidentiality. If your appointments are getting backed up because of this problem, you can always announce "Hey, this is great stuff. Mind if I have Nurse Johnson listen in?" If that doesn't stop the stories, you can always take notes and sell it as books like we do.

Dermatologist

Dermatologists don't lose many patients. It gets dull, certainly, dealing with teenage complexions all day but at least you seldom have to explain to a frantic new widow how her husband's pimple just exploded right in the examining room, and took the better part of his head with it.

Dermatologists spend a lot of time telling patients they have dermatitis, which only the really clever patients realize is a rash, which is what <u>they</u> told the doctor when they walked in.

Calories and the Practice of Medicine

Doctors gain weight and have to watch their calories just like anyone else. Being too busy to keep up a regular exercise schedule, many physicians rely on the following calorie chart to control their girth.

Activity	Calories Burned
Filling out insurance form	18 calories
...if patient changes company	156 calories
...getting paid by patient's new company	732 calories
Handling Medicare forms	52 calories
Handling Medicare & Medicaid	184 calories
Reading Medicare & Medicaid regulations	286 calories
Reading Medicare & Medicaid supplement	491 calories

Calories and the Practice of Medicine

Activity	Calories Burned
Explaining Medicare requirements	142 calories
Explaining why you can't do procedure for Medicare amount	496 calories
...to little old lady	847 calories
Grumbling about insurance & bureaucracy	49 calories
Discussing National health schemes with liberal friends	392 calories
Contemplating return to law school	46 calories

The Malpractice System

U.S. physicians pay nine billion dollars a year in malpractice insurance. I'm not making this up, though most obstetricians you talk to will make you think they pay this much themselves—monthly. The cost of the kind of defensive medicine that doctors are forced to practice exceeds the above sum by a figure that sounds surprisingly like the national debt.

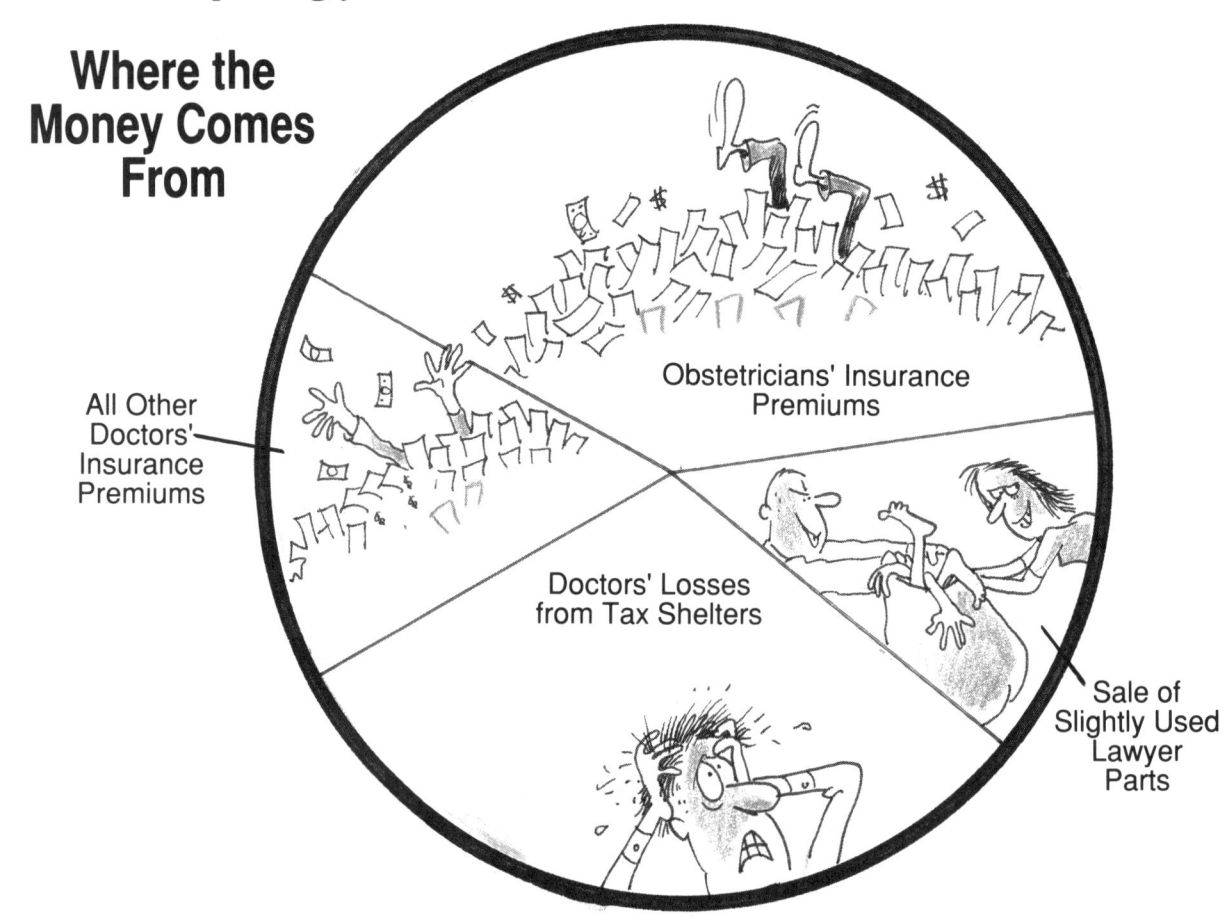

Where the Money Comes From
- Obstetricians' Insurance Premiums
- All Other Doctors' Insurance Premiums
- Doctors' Losses from Tax Shelters
- Sale of Slightly Used Lawyer Parts

The Malpractice System

You can easily see from this chart that legal and administrative fees eat up most of the premium dollars. In fact, if the present growth of the legal profession continues, everyone in the U.S. will be a lawyer by the year 2012.

Where the Money Goes

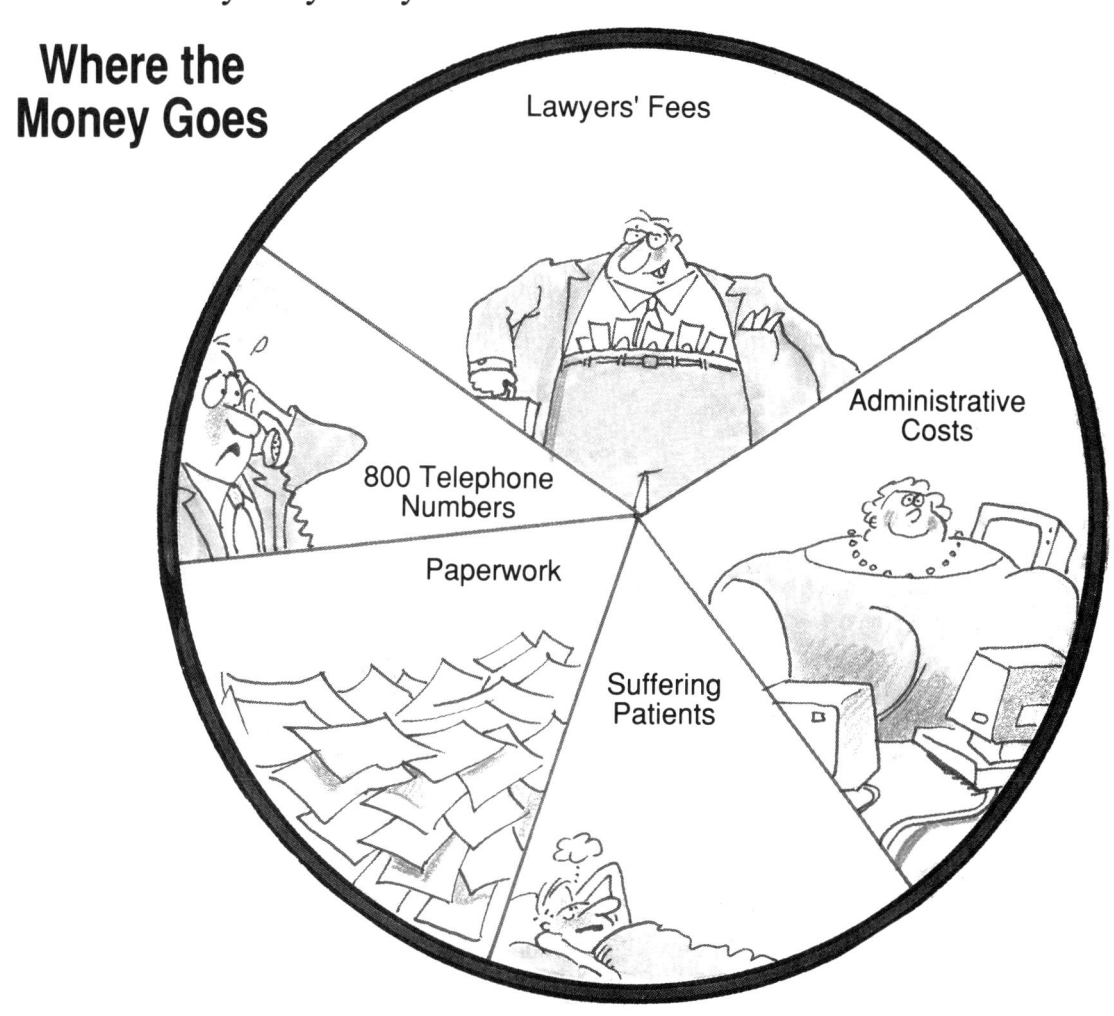

The Patients

Almost every patient has a mental agenda of how they want you to treat them when they enter your office. You'd best fulfill the agenda or they will leave very unhappily. Most examinations and tests are used to ferret out this information. A wise doctor will ask the patient, "Well, Mrs. Van Dorm, how do you think I can help you?" A rich doctor will do just what she suggests. Funny thing is, it almost always makes them better.

Respect for Doctors

Your family won't listen to you and your patients never did. Nurses are an independent lot who have their own way of thinking and doing things that few doctors try to change. The aides and cleaning people get very annoyed when you get in their way, say, to examine a patient or save a life. If it weren't for general anesthesia it'd be a wonder if any medical procedures could be accomplished at all.

Pain in the Butt Patients

They've read a magazine article or some Sunday supplement that tells them how to choose a doctor and control their visit.

These patients:

1. Complain about waiting in the waiting room. Waiting rooms are <u>for waiting</u>, hence the name, so it seems silly to grumble about that.
2. They want <u>your</u> full medical history and they test you on current theories.
3. They prefer to address you by your first name.
4. They will insist on a full explanation of their illness, approximately equal to the course you took in medical school. Then they'll compare your explanation with the three others that they have received from different doctors.

Pain in the Butt Patients

5. They insist on taking copies of all their medical records, along with a selection of the magazines, from the waiting room.

6. You can expect at least 3 follow-up phone calls, unless you've been summarily dismissed by failing one of their earlier tests.

7. You had better hope their insurance is current because they never pay their bills.

10 Commandments of Medicine

I. Thou shalt not recommend broccoli to patients who already fart too much.

II. Thou shalt not giggle when a patient describes sex problems.

III. Thou shalt sign insurance forms only after pretending to peruse them.

IV. Thou shalt not park the new Mercedes in the hospital parking lot.

V. Thou shalt feign interest by exclaiming "Hmmm" and "I see" with every symptom a patient describes.

10 Commandments of Medicine

VI.	Thou shalt remember your struggling resident days whenever you hear complaints on doctors' compensation.
VII.	Thou shalt perform surgery on lawyers using only dull scalpels.
VIII.	Thou shalt avoid all hypochondriacs at parties and social gatherings.
IX.	Thou shalt repeat only the juiciest, confidential secrets to your mate.
X.	Thou shalt not perform unnecessary procedures merely to protect your malpractice insurance, unless the rates increased by more than 12% last year.

These other books are available at many fine store[s]

#2350 Sailing. Using the head at night • Sex & Sailing • Monsters in the Ice Chest • How to look nautical in bars and much more nautical nonsense.

#2351 Computers. Where computers really are made • How to understand computer manuals without reading them • Sell your old $2,000,000 computer for $60 • Why computers are always lonely and much more solid state computer humor.

#2352 Cats. Living with cat hair • The advantages of kitty litter • Cats that fart • How to tell if you've got a fat cat.

#2353 Tennis. Where do lost balls go? • Winning the psychological game • Catching your breath • Perfecting wood shots.

#2354 Bowling. A book of bowling cartoons that covers: Score sheet cheaters • Boozers • Women who show off • Facing your team after a bad box and much more.

#2355 Parenting. Understanding the Tooth Fairy • 1000 ways to toilet train • Informers and tattle tales • Differences between little girls and little boys • And enough other information and laughs to make every parent wet their beds.

#2356 Fitness. T-shirts that will stop them from laughing at you • Earn big money with muscles • Sex and Fitness • Lose weight with laughter from this book.

#2357 Golf. Playing the psychological game • Going to the toilet in the rough • How to tell a real golfer • Some of the best golf cartoons ever printed.

#2358 Fishing. Handling 9" mosquitoes • Raising worms in your microwave oven • Neighborhood targets for fly casting practi[ce] • How to get on a first name basis with the Coast Guard plus even more.

#2359 Bathrooms. Why people love their bathroom • Great games to help pass the tim[e] on toilets • A frank discussion of bathroom odors • Plus lots of other stuff everyone out [of] diapers should know.

#2360 Biking. Why the wind is always agai[nst] you • Why bike clothes are so tight • And lot[s] of other stuff about what goes thunk, thunk, thunk when you pedal.

#2361 Running. How to "go" in the woods • Why running shoes cost more than sneaker[s] • Keeping your lungs from bursting by letti[ng] the other guy talk.

#2362 Skiing. Understanding ski reports • Chair lift etiquette • Why trail maps don't show trees • Where moguls really come from • Rules for hot tubs and saunas

#2363 Doctors. Handling lawyer and insurance problems with a rusty scalpel • Offshore medical schools and conferences • Why surgeons always get to carve the turke[y] on Thanksgiving • And a lot more humor tha[t] can be easily digested between patients.

#2364 Lawyers. Making faces at the judge • Why lawyers make better lovers • Quit law and make more money as a plumber • The fi[rst] lawyer book ever written with more jokes for lawyers than about them.

Ivory Tower Publishing Co., Inc.   125 Walnut St., PO Box 9132, Watertown, MA 02272-9[...]
Telephone #: (617) 923-1111   Fax #: (617) 923-8839